England Picture Book

THE SWAN
THE SWAN
PUB OF THE YEAR 2013
THE SWAN

citi
HSBC

WILDWOOD GRILLS PIZZA PASTA
WILDWOOD
The Old

3 Revolutions
ICE CREAMS

pharmacy
Boots
SEA SOLDIER
DH 16
DARTMOUTH

Printed in Great Britain
by Amazon

48912852R00025